"Can I have chicken nuggets
for three, a vegeburger
and two colas?"
asks one customer.

3

In the kitchen, Ash collects a delivery. "The buns are here!" he calls.

Abdel is preparing the burgers. They take a few minutes to get ready.

BUSY PLACES

Fast Food Restaurant

Carol Watson

W
FRANKLIN WATTS
LONDON·SYDNEY

It's 12 o'clock at McDonald's fast food restaurant.
People are queuing up at the counters to order their favourite food.

Then Jim wraps the burgers in paper and puts them in a heated container which keeps them warm.

Next Jim checks on the french fries.
They take ten minutes to cook
to a golden brown colour.
"These are almost ready," he says.

When the french fries are crisp
Ali puts some salt on them.
Then she uses a scoop to put them into
cardboard cartons.

"Here are the chicken nuggets!" calls another crew member. She uses metal tongs to pick up the hot food.

Then Jim puts the vegeburger into a box to serve.

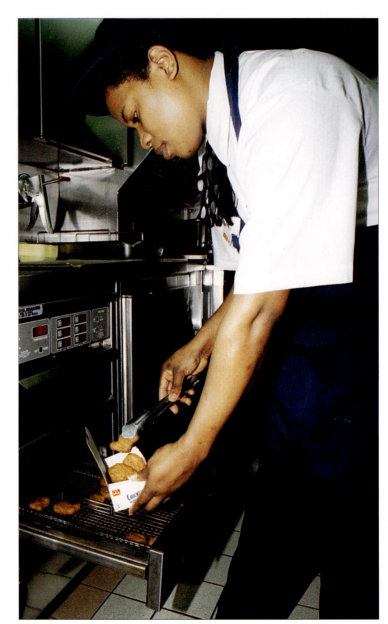

At the drinks machine
John is getting the colas.
He puts some ice into
a cardboard cup and
holds it in position.
Then he presses a button
and the drink comes out.

"Two colas coming up!" says John.
"The food is ready now!"

At 1p.m. the restaurant is very busy.
The tables are full of people eating and chatting together.

Alison talks to her baby. "Do you want a french fry, Jake?" she asks.

11

When the customers leave, crew members wipe the tables and wash the floor.

They work quickly so that the restaurant is always ready for the next customers.

In the kitchen
Ash does some
washing up.

Upstairs there is a birthday party in the children's area. Fergus is five years old and he has invited his friends to celebrate with him.

Martha is the McDonald's party entertainer.
She gives the children hats and aprons
to wear. "Let's do some colouring while we
wait for the food to arrive," says Martha.

Next the children play party games.
They all clap and sing together.

Then some staff arrive
with trays of party meals.
The children sit at their
table and wait to be served.

"Mmm, I'm hungry!" says Fergus.
All the children enjoy their burgers,
french fries and drinks.

Everybody sings "Happy Birthday" as Fergus blows out the candles on his birthday cake.

Then the restaurant staff give the children balloons and "goodie bags" to take home.

At 6 p.m. Kirstie arrives in her car for a take-away meal at the "drive-thru" part of the restaurant.

"A Big Mac, one coffee and a cola, please," she says to the till person. He gives her a napkin and straw.

Next Kirstie drives around
the corner and stops the car
at another window.
Here she pays the bill.

When Kirstie reaches the third window
the manager gives her the food she has ordered.
"Enjoy your meal," he says.
"And have a nice day!"

Care and safety in a restaurant

When you are in a busy place it is important to make sure that you and others keep safe.

Try to remember some of these tips:

1. Don't run around in the restaurant. People may be carrying hot drinks which could spill and burn someone.

2. Tread carefully on any part of the restaurant floor that has just been washed. It is easy to slip on a wet floor.

3. Always stay close to your parent or friend.

4. If you have eaten a "take-away" always put your empty cartons in a litter bin. Never throw them on the floor.

5. At a "drive-thru" restaurant always stay in your car.

Index

© 1998 Franklin Watts
This edition 2002

Franklin Watts, 96 Leonard Street
London EC2A 4XD

Franklin Watts Australia
56 O'Riordan Street
Alexandria, Sydney, NSW 2015

ISBN 0 7496 4570 9 (pbk)

Dewey Decimal Classification 647.9

A CIP catalogue record for this book
is available from the British Library

Printed in Hong Kong

Editor: Samantha Armstrong
Designer: Kirstie Billingham
Photographer: Steve Shott
Illustrations: Richard Morgan

With thanks to staff at McDonald's,
City Road and Putney High Street,
London, Fenella Burns, James
Graham and Helen Cheese-Probert.